Move the Needle

GET PAST THE THINGS THAT HINDER YOUR SUCCESS

JOSEPH K. WILLIAMS SR., MDIV

MOVE THE NEEDLE
Published by Purposely Created Publishing Group™
Copyright © 2020 Joseph K. Williams Sr.
All rights reserved.

No part of this book may be reproduced, distributed or transmitted in any form by any means, graphic, electronic, or mechanical, including photocopy, recording, taping, or by any information storage or retrieval system, without permission in writing from the publisher, except in the case of reprints in the context of reviews, quotes, or references.

Printed in the United States of America
ISBN: 978-1-64484-304-8

Special discounts are available on bulk quantity purchases by book clubs, associations and special interest groups.
For details email: sales@publishyourgift.com
or call (888) 949-6228.
For information log on to www.PublishYourGift.com

Move the Needle

*I find great joy in the love of my family and friends.
They have inspired and encouraged me over the years and
are the central inspiration of this book.*

*At the time of this writing, my mother is suffering from severe
dementia. While her awareness and ability to remember are in
sharp decline, it is important to me to note that she has been my
champion. Ma, you always taught me to be the best that I could
be and to never stop trying. Thank you for teaching me how to be
a persevering, positive, and productive Black man.*

*To the love of my life, Ivey Nycole, who is my muse:
you have demonstrated to me that a true love and
partnership can be had when you are willing to put in the work.
Your encouragement and belief in who I am has helped
me to walk steadily in the face of strong winds.
Our love gives me new energy each day.
Thank you for your patience and persistence.*

*To my children, LaToya, Brianna, Joseph II, Sloane, and Bryce:
you are my joy and reason to keep the flame of inspiration
burning. There are countless others whose names are not written
on this page, but you are nonetheless appreciated dearly. I have
been blessed with a cadre of people who have demonstrated care
and concern and have challenged me to produce this book.
You, too, have inspired me to Move the Needle!*

Table of Contents

Foreword ix
Introduction 1
Section I: Moving Forward 7
    Chapter 1 – Simple-Mindedness 9
    Chapter 2 – Set Discourse 17
    Chapter 3 – Sentiment Shift 23
    Chapter 4 – Supposition Shift 29
    Chapter 5 – Shift to Soundness 37
    Chapter 6 – Single-Minded 45
Section II: Move On Up 53
    Chapter 7 – Be Factual 57
    Chapter 8 – Be Focused 63
    Chapter 9 – Be-Fuddle 69
    Chapter 10 – Be Flexible 75
    Chapter 11 – Move the Needle 83
Sources 89
About the Author 91

Foreword

For thirty-three years, I have known Joe Williams as someone never satisfied with being "stuck." This is in spite of the fact that he's had every reason to be. He could have allowed a challenging upbringing in the tough streets of Ward 8 in Washington, DC, to get him to settle for "stuck." He could have let family turmoil and failed relationships stop him from achieving his goals. He could have accepted "church hurt" and "wickedness in high places," as we say in the church, as reasons not to press on. He could have claimed, rightfully so, that racism and discrimination were the reasons why he only got so far. Joe is someone who qualifies for getting a "pass" if he simply decided to remain satisfied with living life in a stuck position.

But that's not Joe. And that's not who Joe encourages people to be. This powerful, persistent, and profound leader is always exhorting people to "Move the Needle." Joe Williams epitomizes what my uncle Pete used to tell me when turmoil came my way as kid: "It ain't how you fall, it's how you get back up." He is the picture of a man who's had what Gene Rice, our Old Testament professor at Howard University School of Divinity seminary, called "bulldog tenacity." Joe understands what being stuck means—in our personal lives, family lives, and vocational lives. But he also knows how to overcome, and how to overcome through prayer, diligence, determination, and strategic planning. He is a man who by faith and fortitude knows how to turn the sorrows of yesterday into the victories of today and tomorrow for those he serves, and for himself.

For almost ten years, I've been humbled and honored to be Joe's pastor at the Emory United Methodist Church in Washington, DC. Ours has been a great relationship, even though I'm Methodist and Joe is Baptist! Yet, our congregation and I have been incredibly blessed to have him as a part of our preaching team and congregation. His words inform, illuminate, and inspire us all. In this great work, Joe inspires us all to never quit, never give up—God has a great plan for us. With passion and perseverance, we can "Move the Needle" from a place of being stuck to a position of great blessing.

It is this philosophy that has helped encourage "thought leaders," politicians, civic officials, pastors, and congregations all across the country. It is this mindset that inspired the work of many in the private, government, and public sectors of urban and suburban communities. It is this beautiful work that will push someone wondering if they can go on to not only regain passion, but also to proceed with expectation and anticipation that the best of what God has for them is just around the corner.

When Joe preached the "Move the Needle" sermon a few years ago, it was so brilliant that after the benediction, I told him, "that's your book, man. You just laid out the chapters. Now go write!" And write he has!

It is my prayer now that you will read it. If you are someone in the midst of a great challenge in your life—personally and/or vocationally—or if you are stuck and unable to move, this book will bless you, as we say in the church, "real good." It will help you analyze where you are personally and professionally, and systematically and strategically, and with creativity and joy move you to heights unseen.

I am so incredibly proud of my brother and excited for this work. It will help transform the lives of any who know what it means to be stuck, but who demand better for their lives. It's time to get up and "Move the Needle!"

Dr. Joseph W. Daniels, Jr.
Senior Pastor
Emory Fellowship—Washington, DC

Introduction

I have been writing several books for several years, and I am not surprised that my first crack at becoming a published author would be a piece that was born out of trial and testing. I have had many mornings when I just did not feel like pursuing anything. I did not feel like pursuing purpose. I did not feel like pursuing passion. I did not feel like pursuing happiness. I remember standing on the platform of the Metro and watching people going through their commute with war-torn faces, realizing that I was no different—but I knew in my heart that I *should* be different. God had called me to so much more, and yet—with all that I had accomplished in life—I was stuck!

During one of those moments, the drive for this book manifested itself. Like many people in America, I had been mentally consumed by the results of November 2016 and the subsequent results of the first one hundred days of Number Forty-Five. That was a pivotal moment for me. I realized that I was stuck politically, professionally, and personally. I trusted a political system that was not looking out for my best interest and did nothing to push for results in my favor. Professionally, I was coming to the end of my latest "faith iteration"—the charge that God gave me for impact in his kingdom—and could not see my next assignment. Personally, I was saying all the right things, but they were never manifesting into actions that propelled any forward movement.

When I think of the early years of my development, I've found that my environment has been both a catalyst for and a hindrance to my refinement. As a native Washingtonian, I have grown accustomed to being dismissive and being dismissed. Growing up in the southeast quadrant of the District of Columbia (commonly known as East of the Anacostia River), it was easy to develop a chip on my shoulder. I took offense at the low expectations that were both internal and external. When I crossed over to the "other" sections of town, I expected to be dismissed because I was from "Southeast." These internal and external forces have helped to shape my *who*, *when*, and *why* of life. While I have had the fortune of being well read, it was (and always will be) the fortitude of my faith that has provided me the resilience to charge forward, rather than any intellectual prowess. Additionally, a determined personality that will not allow others to speak for me nor dictate how I feel about me has provided me a healthy "wall" for things to roll off. It is with that background that I come to be the author of the pages that follow.

So why this book? This book is to help individuals (like me) to move from the stuck position. I want to share my story, which is imbedded in His-story and in the things that keep us from pursuing Kingdom purposes with a passion and vigor that brings about change. A few years ago, at the Emory United Methodist Church located in the District of Columbia, I preached a sermon with the same title as this book. I was amazed at the number of people who told me how much it helped them and how, when they listened to the CD and reread the notes they captured on that day, they were greatly encouraged. So, I went back and read my notes and listened to the CD—I wanted to see if I could see and hear what they saw and heard. It was then that God showed me that I was to author this book and help to empower people across generations. My personal mission statement is to empower people and communities by guiding them to resources that help them to walk in their power and purpose. In essence, I am doing the thing that is assigned to me during this season.

Move the Needle is about capturing your passion amid internal and external turmoil. What do you do when someone you believed in strongly ends up being an incorrect prognosticator? During the 2016 presidential campaign, former president Barack Obama made it clear that he was confident that the American people would make the wise choice in November by voting for Hillary Clinton. Well, for many Americans the "wise choice" was not the end result. The election of Donald Trump as president was for the most part an unthinkable result. It sent shockwaves throughout every nook and cranny of this country. It paralyzed many people like a deer in headlights. In fact, many people still cannot believe that the existing reality is what it is at the present day. I would submit that people have comparable feelings about Super Bowl LI (the improbable comeback of the New England Patriots over the Atlanta Falcons) and the 2016 election, people are frozen in an emotional prison.

What is my hope? I desire greatly that God will use this book to change the perspective of you, the reader, and help you to move your purpose needle to the forward position. In fact, I want it to have the same impact as public sentiment has upon the development of legislation. I am old enough to remember the time when you could smoke cigarettes in public spaces and places. As public sentiment grew about the effects of secondhand smoke, though, there was a groundswell of voices that resulted in national legislation that altogether halted individuals' ability to light up any form of tobacco on airplanes, in restaurants, or within twenty-five feet of public buildings. I also hope this book will create an internal cooperation that will cause you to rewrite your game plan and put in place the principles that are discussed in the subsequent pages.

I will take an exegetical (an explanation or critical interpretation of a text) look at two passages of scripture that will provide a game plan for your use. The first is 1 Corinthians 13:11 (KJV): "When I was a child, I spake as a child, I understood as a child, I thought as a child: but when I became a man, I put away childish things." The second is Philippians 3:13 (NKJV): "Brethren, I do not count myself to have apprehended; but one thing I do, forgetting those things which are behind and reaching forward to those things which are ahead." The Apostle Paul's letters were written to different communities. The former is a pastoral letter, written to resolve doctrinal and practical problems within the local church. The latter is considered a prison epistle that reveals the timeless message that true joy is to be found through a dynamic personal relationship with Jesus Christ, and it provides an assurance that God is able to turn around circumstances so that they work for our good and His glory. I will provide a hermeneutical (the study of the methodological principles of interpretation for a relative connection) transfer that will be your guide to moving the needle in your life. In fact, I believe that this will help you to move the needle for subsequent generations and communities across the globe!

When I was growing up, music was recorded on wax. I remember an old record player that we had—an RCA hi-fi system with a color television and a record player. I would play an LP or album over and over, repeatedly, at speeds of 33, 45, and 78 RPM! After playing it to no end, the inevitable would happen: the wax would get scratched. Damage could happen to the wax in multiple ways. If I did not handle the wax properly, left it uncovered or handled it carelessly, it would get scratched. To get past the scratched (stuck) place in the song, you had to either touch the head of the needle arm with your fingertip or place a penny on the head of the needle arm to move it to the next place in the song. I believe that God wants you to continue in an even flow of music. He wants you to hear the music without interruption. He wants you to get past the "scratched" position in your life.

If you are like me, you have had too many goals drown in a sea of good intentions. Proverbs 14:22b–23 (NIV) says, "But those who plan what is good find love and faithfulness.

All hard work brings a profit, but mere talk leads only to poverty." I have read Pastor Mark Batterson's book *Draw the Circle: The 40 Day Prayer Challenge* at least twice. He says, "Prayer is the way we let go and let God. Prayer is the way we take our hands off and let God put His hands on. Prayer is the difference between you fighting for God and God fighting for you." It is time to pray. It is time to plan. It is time for you to progress. It is time to profit from your pursuit of all the things that God has shown you over the course of your life. It is time to get off the sidelines and get in the game. It is time to move the needle!

SECTION I
MOVING FORWARD

Chapter 1
Simple-Mindedness
When I was a child . . .

While I don't intend to spend a lot of time dwelling on an overstated issue, I believe it is important to make mention of what I define as the manhood crisis in America. When I was acting out as a teenager (simply put, trying to "be grown"), my mother would say "you are being a *manish-boy*!" That term has stuck with me; it is defined as a male who has the biological and chronological attributes of manhood but has the thinking and behavior of a boy. There are three stages of development for the biological male: **maleness**, **boyhood**, and **manhood**. I define them in this manner: **Maleness** wants what it wants when it wants it and does not consider the inconvenience it causes to others to get what it wants. **Boyhood** is the preparation stage that provides the key ingredients of discipline and life's foundational principles— and how those are taught and learned are crucial to one's development. **Manhood** is understanding the previous two stages through a maturation process that takes on self-responsibility and all assigned obligations of destiny and purpose. Using my mother's phrase, the manhood crisis in America can be attributed to the fact that there are many *manish-boys* masquerading as men. While I give this analogy for men, both men and women have stages and seasons of development. I will refer to this framework throughout the book. It is important to keep in mind the stages and seasons of development if we are going to move the needle in our lives.

I like this quote from the late great Muhammed Ali, from his November 1975 interview published in *Playboy* magazine: "The man who views the world at fifty the same as he did at twenty has wasted thirty years of his life." This statement resonates with me because it speaks to a collection of seasons in life. Certainly, we would agree that we are different (or we should be) at the age of fifty than at the age of twenty! Our lens is different. Our experiences have made us different. The expectation is that we have moved from immaturity to maturity.

In 1 Corinthians 13:11, the Apostle Paul interjects a powerful statement that begins with "When I was a child . . ." While the main theme of the chapter speaks to the quality and characteristics of love, the interjection of verse 11 causes the reader to pause and consider one's disposition or state of being. "When I was a child" speaks to a simple-minded state of being. The Greek word for child is *nepios* (pronounced nay-pee-os), and it literally means a babe, an immature or simple-minded person. To move the needle, we need to make sure that we understand the limitations of this position in life. "When I was a child" says that I have a limited focus and find myself getting into situations that can have a negative impact. I call that "getting into this or that." A limited, immature focus will cause you to move your attention from having purpose to being purposeless. A simple-mindedness approach can have us stuck in a time warp, in a season of life that doesn't require us to move out of our comfort zone—and thus never prompts us to move forward.

When I was in seminary, I dreaded the year I took Greek. It is a language that has no corresponding relation to the English language. There is no comparison. My New Testament professor, the late Dr. Cain Hope Felder, was very fluent in the language, and it was an intimidating experience. I remember a moment during that class when I thought, "I can't graduate and get my degree *until* I learn this language." I was in danger of becoming stuck if I didn't figure my way through Greek! The primary participle *when* implies being stuck or not knowing when to stop. In Greek, the word that is translated into the English word *until* (or 'til) is a function word that indicates continuance to a specified time. I could not get through Greek by throwing a tantrum. I had to devise a plan that included me overcoming my self-induced intimidation (and getting a tutor) so that I could learn the nuances of the language. That proved to not only be a pivotal moment during my seminary experience, it also proved to be a moment for me to use when I faced similar circumstances in life.

If you are walking in uncertainty, you cannot move toward your destiny and the place that God intends for you to occupy. If you are unsure about who you are, you can be sure that you don't know where you are going. My late maternal grandfather would always ask me the question, "Boy, where are you going?" I finally got the nerve to ask him why he always asked me that question. He stated, "Because I always want you to be aware of the direction you are headed."

I am convinced that the only way for me to move from faith to faith is to understand that I can't use a simple-minded approach to life. In the song "Bring Back the Days of Yea and Nay," the Winans sing, "I remember when life was so simple/ You did or you didn't/ You would or you wouldn't/ But it ain't like that anymore." That is the position we must take as we mature. We can't use a simple-minded approach and expect to get to the next level, because life isn't like that anymore. Being simple-minded places you in a deficit position that does not allow your best qualities to rise to the surface. The Apostle Paul, speaking to the Church at Corinth, said, "And I, brethren, could not speak to you as to spiritual people but as to carnal, as to babes in Christ. I fed you with milk and not with solid food; for until now you were not able to receive it, and even now you are still not able" (1 Corinthians 3:1–2 NKJV). I have come to learn that I have had to choose my disposition in life. Nothing has been given to me (outside of God's grace). I learned a short poem during my membership in the Lampados Club of the Omega Psi Phi Fraternity. While there are different variations of the poem, the one we were taught read thusly: "Excuses are tools of the incompetent. They are used to build bridges to nowhere. People who use them become monuments of nothing. Therefore, there are no such things as excuses!" I shared that with my children when they were growing up and use it as a reminder to myself when the urge to operate with simple-minded thinking tries to invade my thought process. I am convinced that you have the same tools in your arsenal and can avoid the snare of simple-mindedness.

The Recapture

Being simple-minded will . . .
Get you caught up in "this and that"
Have you focused on that time
Give you false momentum
Cause you to throw a tantrum
Allow uncertainty to cloud your thought process
Keep you in the position of being unsure
of who you are and where you are going

Chapter 2

Set Discourse

. . . I spake as a child . . .

When Charles Spurgeon died in January 1892, London went into mourning. Nearly 60,000 people came to pay homage during the three days his body lay in state at the Metropolitan Tabernacle. Some 100,000 people lined the streets as a funeral parade two miles long followed his hearse from the Tabernacle to the cemetery. Flags flew at half-staff and shops and pubs were closed. (*Christianity Today*, issue 29, 1991) He was known as the "Prince of Preachers." My study of Spurgeon suggests that, despite this outpouring of grief, in life he had an edge about him that rubbed people the wrong way. In a statement that described his approach for getting nineteenth century Great Britain to hear the Gospel of Christ, Spurgeon said, "I am perhaps vulgar, but it is not intentional, save that I must and will make people listen" (*Spurgeon Morning & Evening Devotionals*, ChristiansUnite.com, January 25, 2017). More than two centuries later, seminarians and theologians are still listening to Charles Haddon Spurgeon. Why? Because Spurgeon knew how to move beyond a set discourse.

The Apostle Paul continues to demonstrate how we can be limited in our individual expression or speech when he states,

"I spake as a child . . ." The word *spake* comes from an obsolete Greek verb (*laleo*, pronounced lal-eh'-o) which means to say, show, or speak. But the word spake also means *lego*, which is a primary verb in Greek that is usually of systematic or set discourse. It implies that the individual is limited based on knowledge and maturity. Do you know people who have a lot to say about nothing? Do you know people who talk just so that they can hear themselves talk? Do you know people whose words or thought processes are limited and lack relevance because they have not spent the necessary time to grow their knowledge base? I have worked with older adults for more than ten years, and in that time I have encountered some individuals that cause me to pause in disbelief. The mindset that some have displayed when it comes to some of the basics of life has been mindboggling. Some of these wonderful individuals have said some things that made me scratch my head!

When the Apostle states "I spake as a child," he is speaking of two things specifically. First, the inference is of one that speaks with the speed of immaturity. When my children were young, I had to teach them the lesson that they could not interrupt people when they were talking. I taught them that they had to say "excuse me" and then wait to be heard. The thought behind the lesson was to teach them that just because they *said* "excuse me," it did not mean that they had a right to interrupt the conversation immediately. When we speak with the speed of immaturity, we are *limited* because we have not given ourselves time to consider all factors involved. Speaking with the speed of immaturity can put us in the position of being labeled *limited* and can consequently dilute our sphere of influence. In the book of James, he states, "My dear brothers and sisters, take note of this: Everyone should be quick to listen, slow to speak and slow to become angry" (James 1:19 NIV). Speaking with the speed of immaturity will cast a shadow on every area of your life.

Have you ever said to someone or to yourself that "people just have to accept me for who I am!?" There was a time in my life when I operated with that mentality as a badge of honor. Over time, however, the Holy Spirit began to show me the flaw of my mindset. I had allowed my disposition to become a set discourse that limited my effectiveness even before I set foot in a room! Let me explain further. When I met my fiancée, early in our relationship she said to me, "It seems that you have a chip on your shoulder." I told her, "I grew up in Southeast DC; it is natural to have a chip on your shoulder when you are labeled because of your environment." Her response to me was, "Maybe early on, but not at your age." I considered her words, and the Holy Spirit said to me, "She's right! Because you are in Christ, you are a new creature. Let the chip go!"

Secondly, the Apostle Paul is suggesting that when we speak as a child, we limit our effectiveness as community leaders. The Greek word harangue means to speak in a forceful or angry way. In my advocacy efforts for older adults, my words were piercing, and people would hate to see me coming. I was respected because of my passion and knowledge but disrespected because of my delivery. It is one thing to be a "fire and brimstone" preacher, but it's another thing to be a consensus builder that dropped concrete slabs on people's heads! My disposition caused me to speak with the speed of immaturity and with a forceful tone. If we want people to hear us, we must let go of the things that negatively inform our thinking and actions. I can always tell when I am "feeling some kinda way," as it can be heard in my intonation. Doesn't that sound like one who is speaking as a child?

We must develop a systematic expression that will break silence properly. As a parent, it is important to have a consistent way you discipline your children—especially when they throw temper tantrums. Anger, frustration, or actions that are birthed from a state of depression are not a systematic expression. Those emotions and/or states of being will not provide you with the consistency that is needed to move forward.

By listening to those whom God has placed in our lives and asking God to perfect our hearts with change, we can move the needle to a greater level of maturity. Proverbs 22:11 says, "One who loves a pure heart and who speaks with grace will have the king for a friend" (NIV). In order to move from a set discourse that limits your effectiveness to one of mature expression, you have to address those areas in your life that limit God's ability to weave his purpose into every fiber of your being.

The Recapture

A set discourse will . . .
Determine what you say
Dictate what you shew people
Cause you to speak with the speed of immaturity
Make you develop a systematic expression that breaks silence properly
Have you speaking in a forceful or angry manner

Chapter 3

Sentiment Shift

. . . I understood as a child . . .

A favorite quote of mine, one often attributed to Mark Twain, states, "When I was a boy of fourteen, my father was so ignorant I could hardly stand to have the old man around. But when I got to be twenty-one, I was astonished at how much the old man had learned in seven years." I shared this quote with my oldest son so often that when he was in college, before I could complete the statement, he said, "You don't have to tell me that anymore! I got it, I got it!"

I like this quote because it indicates that the speaker had an experience with his father that involved a sentiment shift. The Apostle Paul uses the Greek word *phroneo* (pronounced fron-eh'-o), which means to exercise the mind by having a sentiment that points earnestly in a certain direction. Merriam-Webster defines *sentiment* as an attitude, thought, or judgment prompted by feeling, or the emotional significance of a passage or expression as distinguished from its verbal context. It is an exercise of the mind. In the statement "I understood as a child," the Apostle is implying that he had a limited ability because of the state and stage of childhood. The expectations we have of children are far different from the expectations we have of adults. A sentiment shift means that an individual understands that their cognitive faculties need to move from careless and callous to sensitive and sympathetic, combined with an empathetic understanding. It indicates that the art of "being careful" is always in operation in a person's thinking and acting.

Moving to the next level is an important concept to keep in mind for personal growth. For growth to take place inwardly, one must be of one mind or be of the same mind. Philippians 2:5 (KJV) encourages us to "Let this mind be in you, which was also in Christ Jesus." The importance of being of one mind or of the same mind as Christ is vital to our spiritual and social development. An example of this importance can be seen when considering large groups that are trying to work together. I am known for creating dynamic relationships among individuals and organizations. You can say that I am a "networker" of sorts. The most important quality that people and organizations need to work together is a "one mind attitude." The District of Columbia (notice that I did not say Washington, DC) is not known for a "one mind/same mind" spirit. It is quite the opposite. Socially, politically, and religiously, the players in the District want to achieve a common good, but set about to accomplish their goals in a very individualistic manner. The Church community is infamous for displaying a very similar attitude. It is difficult to get twenty clergy in a room to agree to an outcome-based agenda. Why? Because we cannot move to a place of one mind/same mind. Cities and communities are fragmented because of the "large and in charge" mentality. Adults who are selfish and self-centered act like children who never learned that the world does not revolve around them and their desires.

A sentiment shift is necessary to move the needle because it helps us to curb unwise actions and propels us toward a certain direction. I grew up in a family and community in which everyone had a nickname (in fact, there are some people whose government name I do not know to this day). I believe, however, that there comes a time in our lives that we should no longer allow people to refer to us by our nicknames. If people are going to take you seriously, you cannot be known as "Boo-Boo," "Ray-Ray," or "Pookie." In other words, we should insist that people understand that we have matured through curbed actions.

There must be a determination in your mind to alter your course of action and move toward a certain direction—one that leads you to the best position that God has for your life, that leads you to maximizing your gifts and talents and using them to build the Kingdom of God and the community in which you live. I believe it is important for us to ask ourselves the hard questions. It is important that we look at the person in the mirror in a very realistic way—which is from an inside-out perspective. A sentiment shift will cause you to be more careful in your thinking and your actions.

The Recapture

A sentiment shift will cause you to . . .

Be careful
Be of one mind
Be of the same mind
Curb your actions
Move in a certain direction
Shift your cognitive faculties from careless
and callous to sensitive and sympathetic

Chapter 4

Supposition Shift

. . . I thought as a child . . .

Belief systems are ideas or theories that are true to an individual, even with no proof of their validity. Belief systems are important because they are determining factors in how we engage and connect with people and society. Bishop David Perrin is a powerful man of God and one of my mentors, someone who has had Kingdom impact across the globe. He often says, "Be careful how you hear, because it determines how you live." It follows simple logic; you live out what you believe from within, and how you hear a thing influences your interpretation and, thus, what you believe. One of the reasons that men physically abuse women is because they believe that it is the best way to communicate a dominant position. In the same manner, women who verbally abuse men may do so because they believe it is the best way to be in control and heard.

When the Apostle Paul states "I thought as a child," he leads us into what I define as a "supposition shift." Proverbs 23:7a (NKJV) says, "For as he thinks in his heart, so is he." When a supposition shift is in operation, your reasoning and reckoning move toward a level of maturity. There is a stark difference in the thinking of a twelve-year-old and a twenty-two-year-old (or least there should be). It is expected that the two would ask fundamental questions from a different frame of reference. In fact, as you age, you are no longer the subject of your own discourse. When our reasoning and reckoning matures, we begin to understand the true meaning of Logos (the written Word of God). The Divine reason implicit in the cosmos brings true order, and gives our hearts form and our minds meaning.

In their book entitled *Becoming Married*, authors Herbert Anderson and Robert Cotton make the following statement: "If a couple and/or their families are determined to make a new family just like the old ones, then it is difficult for God to be doing a new thing." Likewise, if our reasoning and reckoning does not mature, our progress is limited and our growth is stunted.

A supposition shift also involves how we talk and how we manage our intonation. A child is expected to talk like a child. But an adult is expected to have a thorough and reasonable discussion of a subject. Throwing a temper tantrum during a conversation is not the best way to get a point across. Likewise, badgering a person amid a conversation is also ineffective and childish.

The United States is amid a crisis because we have not moved the needle on racism. Dr. Cornell West, in a chapel service at Howard University in 2017, said,

> The country is in deep trouble. We've forgotten that a rich life consists fundamentally of serving others,

trying to leave the world a little better than you found it. We need the courage to question the powers that be, the courage to be impatient with evil and patient with people, the courage to fight for social justice. In many instances we will be stepping out on nothing, and just hoping to land on something. But that's the struggle. To live is to wrestle with despair, yet never allow despair to have the last word.

When the set leader is incapable of conducting conversations with a proper intonation, it will put a country or society into a tailspin. These United States will continue to be the divided states until there is a supposition shift. The Administration of the Forty-Fifth President has increased the division racially, socially, and economically. The only way to change the course of this nation and our lives collectively is to make a supposition shift at the voter box!

The next aspect of a supposition shift involves the intent of our word and the effort of our work. Your word and work go hand in hand. A child must be taught how to place proper value on their words. I have five children (three girls and two boys), and I will tell you (as would any parent) that it is critical to instill within them the importance of placing value on their words. There is truth to the statement "you are what you say." As a child, I would often say the first thing that came to mind—without thinking about the relevance or connection. When that happened in the presence of my grandfather, he would quip, "it was okay until you opened your mouth and removed all doubt!"

It is very irritating to be in a conversation with someone who does not think before they speak. That is a clear picture of a person who does not recognize the importance of their words or the meaning of a supposition shift in their lives. It is vital for individuals in leadership to weigh their words carefully—and the people who can weigh their words are the people who get beyond the stuck position in their lives.

While the value we place on our words is important to a supposition shift, our work is equally important. I take issue with lazy people. Laziness only produces unhealthy and unproductive individuals who become codependent upon systems, society, and services. On the mirror in my bathroom, I have the following proverb on a three by five card that I read every morning and every night: "But those who plan what is good find love and faithfulness. All hard work brings a profit, but mere talk leads only to poverty" (Proverbs 14:22b–23, NIV). A good work ethic causes a supposition shift in your life because of the experience gained from your efforts. Hard work brings a profit! Mere talk leads to poverty! Church folk would say that you are tinkling brass and a sounding cymbal. The late James Brown would say that you are "talkin' loud and saying nothing"! If you want to achieve God's best for you, then you must be willing to have a supposition shift in your life. Boldly declare, "Your word I have hidden in my heart . . ." (Psalm 119:11a, NKJV).

The praise and worship group Higher Praise released a song in the eighties with these lyrics:

Set me on fire oh Lord

I want to live my life

To please you in every way

Set me on fire once more

So that the world can

Watch me burn for you!

Allow God to be the Revealer, and let his revelation in Jesus Christ bring you to a supposition shift that will set the world on fire!

The Recapture

A supposition shift will cause you to change your . . .

> Reasoning
> Reckoning
> Talk
> Intonation
> Word
> Work

Chapter 5

Shift to Soundness

. . . but when I became a man . . .

In many ways, I consider my late father to be the epitome of manhood. In fact, I attribute my attitude toward work to my observance of his work ethic. He had a high school education and an entrepreneurial spirit. After spending years working for companies, he set out to start his own trash removal company. In fact, in the early seventies, one of his clients was a children's hospital in the District of Columbia (that was huge for an African American-owned small business). I learned from him that being a man was about being consistently responsible, being constantly robust, and being continually receptive of information and knowledge.

A shift to soundness happens when an individual has first learned to tame their own "-ness." -Ness is a suffix that indicates state, condition, or quality. A person tames their "-ness" when they have learned discipline through their development process and allow the results to translate to being responsible for their actions. Jesus said in Mark 3:25 (NKJV), "And if a house is divided against itself, that house cannot stand." The shift to soundness—simply put—means that one moves away from unsound actions that cause internal division.

There are four aspects to discover from the Apostle Paul's statement "when I became a man." The first aspect is that it creates a need to rise. The phrase suggests moving and evolving. It is unsound to allow circumstances, situations, and people to keep you down. We are called to get up and keep it moving! A poet by the name of Catherine M.F. Camarda in her poem *Arise* states,

> Arise you who walk among the dead;
>
> Arise, and hold up your hands and head.
>
> Do not allow your Spirit in darkness to sleep.
>
> Do not allow your conscience to have running feet.

The second aspect of the shift to soundness involves being sure that you are always assembled. I have a great-aunt who is an example of always being assembled and/or put together. No matter when I visit this ninety-five-year-old picture of vibrant beauty, she is always well put together. I remember on one occasion, when she was in the hospital, I made my way to visit her in Newark, Delaware. Based on what was shared regarding her condition, I was expecting to see an aging woman, weak and frail. Not my aunt! When I arrived, I found a woman of elegance sitting in her hospital bed with a head wrap on and a matching garment over top of the hospital gown. What she said will always stick with me: "I might be sick, but I don't have to look sick." How many times do we allow our circumstances to determine our disposition? We are called to a higher level!

Jesus said in Matthew 6:16a (NKJV), "Moreover, when you fast, do not be like the hypocrites, with a sad countenance. For they disfigure their faces that they may appear to men to be fasting." If your desire is to move the needle, then you don't want to display to the world that you are immersed in a struggle. I believe that you should have an accountability partner with whom you can share your intimate struggles, a husband, wife, brother, sister, etc. But you don't want to be known as the "woe is me" person! Immature people perpetuate drama, while mature people deal with their issues. Don't be duped by the devil, as growing up is a part of life, growing up in God is a part of your life in Christ.

The third aspect of a shift to soundness is what I like to call "being found." Have you ever noticed how people get lost when things are not going well for them, but are always around when life is grand? Now, I believe firmly that if you're going to focus on moving the needle, then you should do what is necessary to be successful. Let me explain. During my undergraduate tenure at the University of the District of Columbia, I was a single parent and full-time student and worked twenty hours a week during semesters. I had friends who were just full-time students and could always "hang out." I longed to hang out, but had responsibilities that limited my time. During one of my "pouting moments," my mother said something to me that has stuck with me since that time. She said, "The party will always go on. You may think that you are missing out on the fun, but you're not. When you reach your goal and go back to the party, you will find that nothing will have changed. The music and the people will still be there." Although I was not at the party, I could be found. I could be found in the library. I could be found giving the necessary time as a father to my daughter. I could be found at my position at the Veterans Administration. In other words, I did not disappear. Many people allow circumstances to run them off life's stage and consequently push them away from their purpose. Do not shut down your Twitter account because you don't want to hear communications from irritating individuals. Simply block their feed! In fact, the Prophet Isaiah gives a prescription to being found: "Enlarge the place of your tent, and let them stretch out the curtains of your dwellings; do not spare; lengthen your cords, and strengthen your stakes" (Isaiah 54:2, NKJV).

The fourth aspect to a shift to soundness is to be determined to find fulfillment within yourself. As stated previously, this portion of the text indicates that the Apostle is speaking of arriving and evolving at the same time. He realizes his state, but also realizes that his state or position calls for him to be at a different level of maturity. I have found that a key to finding fulfillment within yourself is having the willpower to focus on who you are versus who you are not. When you are in a broken state, broken world, or broken condition, you can become overwhelmed by brokenness. Brokenness will lead you to seemingly be unfulfilled because of the strong winds of dissatisfaction that blow over your life. Do not allow the strong winds of dissatisfaction to cause you to turn away from your faith. You have been ordained by God to be the head, and not the tail; to be the top, and not the bottom. Instead, recall how the power of Christ has brought you a level of satisfaction through other challenges.

God knows that we are not going to be happy with everything, but we can find happiness in everything. Finding fulfillment during a stuck moment is an opportunity to disturb your mind and allows God to use the moment to put our attention in the right place. A prayer of unknown origin that is sometimes attributed to the English sea captain Sir Francis Drake starts, 'Disturb us, Lord, when we are too well pleased with ourselves, when our dreams have come true because we have dreamed too little, when we arrived safely because we sailed too close to the shore." Sometimes, to move us past the pain of our present predicament, God has to disrupt the mindset of our haunting past. God will disturb us out of the thicket that seeks to keep us in a "caught up" mentality.

The Recapture

A shift to soundness will cause you to . . .
Arise
Be Assembled
Be Found
Be Fulfilled

Chapter 6

Single-Minded

. . . I put away childish things.

All of us, at one time or another, have had the challenge of maintaining our focus. I do not know about you, but I have so many balls up in the air, I sometimes forget their priority and lose focus. When we lose focus, it does not necessarily mean that we "lose focus;" it may simply mean that we place our focus somewhere else. I have a friend who can never finish what she starts. She is super talented and smart, but loses focus quickly. She comes up with great business ideas and galvanizes support and buy-ins. Then, somewhere along the way, her attention shifts to a new project. She has so many unfinished ideas that family and friends have grown weary of her "new ideas." My friend cannot develop her ideas because she will not allow time to focus on their completion.

One of the areas in my life that I have had success in is time management. I have learned to squeeze the maximum out of a day. As a badge of honor, I would boldly declare, "I am burning the candle at both ends and the middle!" As a senior pastor and as an executive director (thankfully the positions were not held simultaneously), I would be going from sunup to sundown. I remember sitting in a Board of Directors meeting once and hearing a board member state, "He is sure meeting with a lot of people." The thought occurred to me that I was having many meetings, but I was without a single-minded focus. I was doing great with time management. But where I was placing my energy was being displaced.

I like literature and am drawn to figures whose lives have made an impact in a variety of areas. One such individual is George Washington Carver, a botanist, inventor, and professor. He is known for the work he did with the development of the peanut around the turn of the twentieth century. Did I mention that Carver was also a man of faith? It was said that he would get up at four in the morning, walk through the woods, and have a talk with God with a focus on Job 12:7–8 (I encourage you to stop and read this text before continuing). He would ask God many questions. The story goes, in Carver's own words:

> I said, "Lord why did you make the universe?" The Lord replied: "Ask for something more in proportion to that little mind of yours." "Then why did you make the earth, Lord?" I asked. "Your little mind still wants to know far too much," replied God. "Why did you make man, Lord?" I asked. "Far too much. Far too much. Ask again," replied God. "Explain to me why you made plants, Lord," I asked. "Your little mind still wants to know far too much." So I meekly asked, "Lord why did you make peanuts?" And the Lord said,

"For the modest proportions of your mind, I will grant you the mystery of the peanut." (Excerpt taken from *Overcoming Flaws and Faults of the Human Nature* by Roderick Aguillard.)

Did you notice that God moved his inquiry to a single-minded focus so that Professor Carver could utilize his giftedness in the place where it was well suited? It is a valuable lesson for us all. The Carver story and "I put away childish things" have strong similarities. There are four relational aspects to being single-minded. Let me explain.

First, when you put away childish things, it suggests that you *cease* from being immature. I can only imagine that George Washington Carver's prayer life had matured through his walks and talks with God in the early morning hours. He had come to a place where he understood that there are things that he could give his attention to, and that he was to leave the God things to God. A mature outlook will cause you to cease from putting your energy in the wrong place.

Secondly, the way to develop a single-minded approach is to no longer *cumber* your thought process. Looking at Carver's prayer walk/talk with God in the woods, he realized that while he was seeking truth and insight, he, himself, was the hindrance and obstruction to gaining knowledge. We are called to put away those things that create burdens in our lives. Notice that God's interaction with Carver called for an action from Carver. Often, we ask God to "take it away," while God is calling on us to "put it away." When Joshua was agonizing over the defeat of the Israelites at Ai, God's response was: "So the Lord said to Joshua: 'Get up! Why do you lie thus on your face?'" (Joshua 7:10 NKJV). In other words, put it away and move forward.

Next, we are challenged to destroy displacement by understanding what it means to be *in place and in time*. If you allow a teenager to play video games or watch television without structure, they will do so until it is all-consuming. That is the operation of an immature mind. When the Apostle Paul states "I put away childish things," he is declaring that he has matured to the point of being in the proper position (place) and understanding the appropriate seasons (time). If you are not in the habit of understanding the time and place of your life, you will not be able to maintain single-mindedness. I am in no way suggesting that you cannot do more than one thing at a time. I am suggesting that you have to grow to the place where you can know your capacity (or lack thereof) and capability to be a forward thinker who maintains focus so that you can see it through. There is a stanza in Edgar A. Guest's poem "See It Through" that I always remember:

> When it's vain to try to dodge it,
>
> Do the best that you can do;
>
> You may fail, but you may conquer,
>
> See it through!

When you are single-minded, you complete each assignment and see it through. I believe this firmly: God cannot birth the next thing in you if you lack the ability to maintain your focus and complete what He has assigned to your hands.

The fourth aspect of being single-minded is to know how to *destroy* the things that cause major disruptions in your life. I have watched many people struggle because they lacked the maturity to destroy things in their lives. I am certain you have seen it also: the people you know and love who blame others for the problems in their lives. On so many occasions, we have found ourselves out of position for that very reason. I had a conversation with someone who has shared ministry with me within the church and the community. This individual shared with me that they had recently had a severe medical challenge because of stress. I was struck by what they had determined to be the root cause: work and family. It was not that these areas being a source of stress was surprising, but rather it was the way in which they were having an impact upon the life of that individual. On the family side, the stress was from having unreal expectations of adult children. On the work side, it was from not realizing that their position called for an ability to handle a tremendous workload. Their operating internal mechanism was focused on family and work, and not focused on destroying a systematic attitude that was at the root of the problem.

If you are not willing to deal with the source and the symptoms, you will never be healed from the sickness. If your doctor gives you specific instructions and you ignore them, you will more than likely end up with an unhealthy result. If you are going to maintain a single-minded disposition, you will have to destroy the attitudes and habits that keep you from successful outcomes.

The Recapture

Being single-minded will cause you to . . .
Cease
Cumber
Be in place and in time
Destroy

SECTION II
MOVE ON UP

During my childhood (and that does not seem that long ago to me), there were many wonderful television shows that were accompanied by great theme songs. One such show was *The Jeffersons*. The theme song "Movin' on Up" from that show is repeated musically, and lines from it are used in movies, even in the present day. During that time, there was also a soulful R&B artist by the name of Curtis Mayfield who had a song called "Move on Up" that was not as popular, but was quite inspiring. I find that all of the lyrics of the song are powerful, but the first stanza emphasizes the true meaning:

> Hush now child, and don't you cry
>
> Your folks might understand you, by and by
>
> Just move on up, toward your destination
>
> Though you may find from time to time
>
> Complication

In the original release, Mayfield's intro had so much energy and power that he did not use the bridge until the end of the song. He embedded the "hook" (Move on Up) in each verse with an octave emphasis that empowered the hearer to move from success to success. To move the needle, you must move on up. The way to avoid being a "deer in the headlights" is to not allow your past (good or bad) to define who you are presently. Let us explore how moving the needle and moving on up are simultaneous tasks.

Chapter 7

Be Factual

Brethren, I do not count myself to have apprehended . . .

Philippians 3:13 calls us to pause and consider what it means to move on up. Some people are challenged when it comes to sticking to the facts. All of us at one time or another have added "color" to a story, situation, or circumstance. When an individual is not happy with their lives, being factual does not provide the glamour or glitter or make their lives shiny. In contrast, something that jumps out in this verse is that the Apostle Paul has made an honest assessment of himself.

There are three emphases that come out of the first portion of the verse. The first emphasis says that to maintain a factual position, you must remain relational. Although he spoke from an apostolic position, he made it clear that his position did not make him superior in the eyes of God. It is important to be an individual that can relate to everyone. Not just your family, friends, and people in your fellowship—but even those individuals with whom your associations are not as frequent as they were once before. Not long ago, I lost a first cousin to an illness. I got a call from my aunt and she asked if I would deliver the eulogy. As I prayed and asked God in what manner I should deliver the message of salvation through Christ, he was very clear to me during that time. He said, "Deliver my son as the one who relates to everyone, no matter their station in life." My pastor (who licensed and ordained me) was there, and said to me at the end, "You were the only one who could deliver that message relationally." It is important to be factual within yourself so that you demonstrate the ability to relate to people.

Secondly, in this verse the Apostle Paul demonstrated the ability to reason with himself. How many times have you heard someone say something that just did not come off as sound reason, that just didn't make any sense? The Administration of the Forty-Fifth President appears that way on a consistent basis. When you can be honest with yourself, you will have reason in your view and in your voice. I love the line in William Shakespeare's *Hamlet*, in act 1, scene 3, "To thine own self be true." It is Polonius' last piece of advice to his son Laertes, who is in a hurry to get on the next boat to Paris, where he'll be safe from his father's long-winded speeches. It is something that we all must hold to if we want to continue a life of progress. It is okay to maintain a level of reality. In fact, I share with people that you should "keep it real" because it allows God to demonstrate to you how real He is—in all things.

The third emphasis on being factual is maintaining the expectation to receive something. This is one of the keys to continued growth as an individual. When you realize that you have not "apprehended," it means that there are opportunities, occasions, and openings that you will have a chance to pursue!

Be Factual

When you open yourself to dealing with the facts in your life, you grant God the opportunity to show you the benefits of a life of faith. In his book *The Necessity of Strangers: The Intriguing Truth about Insight, Innovation, and Success*, Alan Gregerman discusses the importance of this mindset. In his discussion, Gregerman quotes from Carol S. Dweck's book *Mindset: The New Psychology of Success*, saying,

In a growth mindset, people see their qualities as things that can be developed through their dedication and effort. Sure they're happy if they're brainy or talented, but that's just the starting point. They understand that no one has ever accomplished great things—not Mozart, Darwin, or Michael Jordan—without years of passionate practice and learning.

I firmly believe that the combination of passion and practice will lead to an earnest expectation. A mindset of being factual will lead you to a powerful truth: "I can do all things through Christ who strengthens me" (Philippians 4:13 NKJV).

When I watch movies, I pay attention to and remember the little lines from the characters. When you join in with the Psalmist and declare, "God, investigate my life; get all the facts firsthand" (Psalm 139:1, MSG), God will use the line that the character Professor Xavier uses in the movie *X-Men*. He says to Magneto, "There is more good in you, Eric, I know there is." No matter what you are facing, you have to know that there is more good inside of you, and God will bring it out of you for His good.

The Recapture

Being factual will cause you to . . .
Be relational
Operate within reason
Maintain the expectation to receive

Chapter 8

Be Focused

. . . but one thing I do . . .

In chapter six I covered the need to develop a single-minded approach as a way to move the needle. That approach has to do with keeping your eye on the goals and objectives that are necessary to propel you forward and out of your stuck position. Here, I want to help you to come to an understanding of what it truly means to be focused. One of the definitions for focus is that it is the adjustment for distinct vision so that an area may be seen distinctly or resolved into a clear image. The word is best understood when it is used in a present progressive tense: I am focusing. When you are in a stuck position, though, it is impossible to put that definition into motion. Proverbs 4:25 (GW) says, "Let your eyes look straight ahead and your sight be focused in front of you." When you are stuck or bogged down by the winds of adversity, you can easily lack distinct vision.

There is a wonderful church mother at Emory Fellowship who is a tremendous blessing and a powerful presence. She is always encouraging people and providing statements with a level of truth in love. One statement she has said is,

"What comes before one? Zero! So, put first things first and last things never!"

There are four elements that describe what it means to be focused. The first element to being focused is maintaining concentration on the "one" thing. In his book *Chazown: Discover and Pursue God's Purpose for Your Life*, Craig Groeschel says, "Everyone ends up somewhere, but few people end up somewhere on purpose." I believe that there is much truth to his statement. When you cannot give full attention to the "one thing," you will find yourself spinning your wheels on many things. I mentioned my friend earlier who has had many stops and starts as she constantly has new ideas. Again, that is because she lacks the ability to put first things first and last things never. I once heard someone say, "The difference between the truth you know and the truth you live equals the pain that you experience." Giving attention to the primary will lead you to reaching beyond the break to bring vision and clarity to your life.

The second element to maintaining a focus is best understood from the Greek translation of the word *one*. In this case, the word *one* relates to the word *only*, or having a single-hearted focus. How many adults do you know who grew up as an only child? You may have found that even at their present age, many of them have the expectation of being the center of attention. On a more personal level, when I think about the most successful moments in my life, I can identify that I had an "only" focus. When I lost more than forty pounds, it was because my mind and heart focused on developing a healthy body. When I met Ivey Nycole, who is now my fiancée, I had to make the decision that she would be my "only" (especially if I wanted to be in her life). God has given each of us free will and the ability to give attention to those things that propel us into our purpose. Groeschel says, "Keep your heart aimed toward [God's] heart and purpose; with time you'll hit his target ever more accurately." When you focus on the "only," your dreams will overtake you and you will begin to have visions of your purpose with regularity and clarity.

The third element of maintaining your focus can be found from hearing what the Apostle Paul does *not* say in the statement "but one thing I do." What he does not say is to give your attention to "other" things. In this context, *other* represents distractions. Distractions come in a variety of forms, shapes, and sizes (and people). Sometimes distractions are real-life challenges that will make you want to stay in bed and pull the covers over your head. The loss of a job, the loss of a loved one, a devastating relationship breakup, or an election that did not go as you thought it would—these things can serve as real-time distractions and cause you to stay in your stuck position. I am in no way making light of life's challenges, but if you want to move the needle, you are going to have to fight the "other" winds that blow in your life. Jesus said in John 16:33b (KJV), "In the world ye shall have tribulation: but be of good cheer; I have overcome the world."

The fourth element of maintaining focus is understanding a simple approach that I define as the "one by one" approach. You may have heard the joke, "How do you eat an elephant? One bite at a time." That is the message behind this element of being focused. It involves systematically undertaking portions instead of multiple aspects of your circumstances. I have learned from people who are good with financial matters that the concept of building wealth is like building a patio with stones. You must lay one at a time. If you expect to move the needle, you need to set goals and work to accomplish them one by one. You cannot allow yourself to become overwhelmed by the big picture. On a whole it is overwhelming, but one by one you can measure progress. I heard a story once about a frog that was merrily hopping his way through a field. One hop landed him in a giant hole. He found out quickly that he did not have the ability to hop his way out of his predicament. For a while he sat there and planned his demise. He figured that the elements or nature were going to overtake him eventually. But he then decided that if he were going to die, he would die trying. So, he kept trying to get out of the hole, and after focusing on that goal with one hop at a time, he eventually succeeded. When he landed back in the field, he decided to look back in the hole. He was astonished at what he saw: a pile of dirt at the bottom of the hole that he had unknowingly added to after each failed hop, until finally it was high enough for him to get out. One by one, each hop got him to a position of success.

The Recapture

Being focused will cause you to . . .
Put first things first and last things never
Maintain an only position (a single heart)
Avoid other (distractions)
Move one by one

Chapter 9

Be-Fuddle

... forgetting those things which are behind ...

One of the most paralyzing positions of people who are stuck is derived from being consumed by their past. Past mistakes will cause you to not try. Past choices will cause you to second guess yourself. On the flip side, you can also become stuck from living off past accomplishments. I can't tell you the number of occasions when I have reconnected with someone from my high school days, and thirty seconds into the conversation they begin to talk about an accomplishment from thirty years ago as if it happened yesterday. Your past mistakes and your past accomplishments can both hold you back, but they can also both be platforms to propel you into the new space where God is taking you. Howard Thurman in his book *The Inward Journey* said, "In whatever sense this year is a new year for you, may the moment find you eager and unafraid, ready to take it by the hand with joy and gratitude."

I like to play golf. I am a competitive individual. I have learned two important lessons in playing golf. The first is that I do not play against those in my foursome; I play the course. Secondly, I must forget my score from hole to hole, good or bad. Why? A good score will cause you to forget the intangibles of the present hole and a bad score will frustrate you into not thinking about what is needed to achieve success on the current hole. What I have found helpful in placing my past into the proper perspective is in this text: "forgetting those things which are behind." And that brings me to the title of this chapter—"Be-Fuddle." While befuddle is a transitive verb, be-fuddling is an intransitive verb that speaks to the act of maintaining perplexity in the mind of the enemy and your detractors. What past failures are you holding on to? What past successes are you still living off? How do you put this into action and make it a vibrant part of your core? It's be-fuddling!

To put this element into play, you need to learn the art of putting less emphasis on "those things." The enclitic (by definition) is a word pronounced with little emphasis. So, to accomplish this feat, one must be enclitic regarding the wrong direction. The Apostle Paul makes a point of placing a strong emphasis on the direction you should be facing, as opposed to facing "those things," when he states, "those things which are behind." It is important to place little emphasis on those things that happened yesterday, last week, last month, or last year! At some point, you must allow the power of God within you to help you gain control over the hurts, pains, and failures that have crippled your progress.

Just as it is challenging to walk up a down escalator, it is challenging to make progress while looking backward. It is one thing to speak of things that are not as though they are, but it is a different thing entirely to speak of those things that are as though they are not! That is the essence of this principle. To look in the face of an adversity that is combined with crippling circumstances, and speak truth to power. That is be-fuddling! This is the power that causes an unemployed person to work in a volunteer capacity as if it is paying top dollar! This is the power that causes a person with a stage four diagnosis of cancer to live their life as if they are cancer-free and beat the doctor's prognosis! The prophet Isaiah says it best: "Do not remember the former things, nor consider the things of old" (Isaiah 43:18 NKJV).

Another important aspect of this principle is that you and I are being charged to literally "lose [those things] out of mind." There is a reckoning that is necessary if you want to make progress. Dr. Ian Smith says in his book *Super Shred: The Big Results Diet*, "Because time is limited, you really need to hit the ground running. Each day you stick to the program is one day you get closer to your goal. Each day you overeat, skip more than one meal, or eat food that's not on the daily menus is considered a slip, and it takes you backward, away from your goal." While I know he is talking about the discipline of maintaining nutrition habits, it can also be used more generally when talking about discipline in maintaining a principle. Discipline and responsibility are important elements for character development. I often say that there is no way around the weight of responsibility that is life on this side of the resurrection. In order to "forget those things which are behind," there has to be a determination and a daily discipline that keeps your eyes on the prize!

Let me discuss one more important element of the be-fuddling principle. There is an underlying power behind the simple words "forgetting those things which are behind." There is a superimposition of time, place, and order. Now that is the power of God, knowing that God has laid a veil over your past in such a manner that no time, place, or order can interrupt the purpose and plan that He has for your life. When you infuse your faith with this fact, there is nothing and no one that can keep you from creating distance from those things that are behind. Mark Batterson says, "As Christ-followers, we are called to take a why not approach to life. It's an approach to life that dares to dream. It's an approach that's bent toward action. And it doesn't look for excuses not to do something." It's time to confuse your circumstance, the enemy, and your haters. Start be-fuddling them!

The Recapture

Be-fuddling will cause you to . . .
Let go of your past
Speak truth to power
Understand God's power that works in you
Understand the superimposition process

Chapter 10

Be Flexible

". . . and reaching forward to those things which are ahead"

We have discussed a variety of points to help you to move the needle in your life, circumstances, and situation. One of the most important things that I have come to realize when I am faced with trying circumstances, ones that challenge my faith and that make me want to cover my head and close my eyes, is the need for faith that is wrapped in flexibility.

I recently went through a period where I lacked consistent income resources. Was I working? Yes. But the positions did not generate consistent income. This season lasted for two years. As I tried to figure out what the Lord was saying to me, I found myself being stretched in ways that I had never experienced. I have been described as a "man's man." I take very seriously the responsibility of being the provider, protector, and prayer warrior in my home. When I could not provide for my family financially, it sent my mental approach into a tailspin. Of course, I asked God what the lesson was that I was to learn—and one of His responses to me was that I needed to develop flexibility in my faith. It was a time that God used to stretch me and to push my faith to the next level. I can tell you that there were days that I felt defeated, deflated, and down. I questioned myself and, yes, I questioned God.

To be flexible (by definition) is to be characterized by a ready capability to adapt to new, different, or changing requirements. I believe strongly that the Apostle Paul is speaking in the same vein when he said ". . . and reaching forward to those things which are ahead." It requires you and I to have the understanding that our flexibility is from a point of strength and not from a point of weakness. There are three aspects of being flexible that I would like to share with you.

The first characteristic of being flexible lies in your presence. There is an expectation of the believer in Christ to have an assertive effort of faith that belies our disposition. We must remember that faith is a weapon, and weapons belong to warriors. Our faith is to be used as a weapon as we engage in spiritual warfare. As an executive director of a nonprofit organization, I had the responsibility of raising funds for the mission. Whenever I would have to meet with a potential funder, I would be sure to dress well. When people would comment on my appearance, I would share that it was important for me to have the presence of someone who at least looked like I had money. I have said this earlier, and it is worth repeating: you cannot allow your circumstances to determine your disposition. As much as I am not a fan of clichés, it is okay to "fake it until you make it." It is during your time of trial that you must believe that your faith is taking you somewhere. As much as we would like to think that we oversee our lives, we must trust and believe that God is in control. We must believe that "all things work together for good" (Romans 8:28b NKJV). I remember reading Tony Dungy's book *Quiet Strength: The Principles, Practices, and Priorities of a Winning Life* and being blown away by the portrayal of his presence and character. In the book, he discusses an experience as a high school athlete that took place during a meeting with the head football coach and an administrator of the school:

> After the meeting, he [the administrator] took me aside and said, "Coach is the coach, and you're the player, and there are times in life when you're going to have to do certain things. That's just how it goes. That's a lesson you're going to have to learn to get through life.

To get through this moment and develop a greater flexibility of faith, you will have to maintain a presence that is reaching forward.

The second characteristic of being flexible is what I call a Williams word (I maintain that if Webster can make up words, so can Williams). The word is purposefore. It is purpose combined with a first-thing-first mentality and last-thing-never disposition. The text says, "reaching forward to those things." It denotes a certain focus and insight to know that there is little wiggle room in the moment to deviate from the lesson God has for you to learn. Being flexible is to allow God's purpose to be your purpose. It is being intentional about getting off the merry-go-round. As a child, I never liked the merry-go-round. It did not excite me at all. As an adult, I have found that I have spent too much time on the merry-go-round because I lacked flexibility of faith in God. Whether we want to admit it or not, we find ourselves stuck because of our own stubbornness. Because we failed to plan, we planned to fail. All too often, we decide that that lack of planning has now become someone else's fault. We play the blame game. Purpose gets thrown out the window and we settle into the role of the victim. But since God has called you to be the victor and not the victim, you must develop flexibility in your faith that focuses on his purpose for your life. Mark Batterson says, "Our failure to act on what we know God is calling us to not only breeds doubt and discouragement; it's a form of disobedience." Operate with purposefore and watch the needle move in your life!

The third characteristic of being flexible is simple. To be flexible, you must be willing to put forth an effort—especially when you *don't feel like it*. Did I mention the fact that there were days when I felt like quitting? Guess what I learned through my experience? Quitting is not an option. We see this characteristic when looking at this scripture from a literal perspective: "and reaching forward to those things *which are ahead*." If you put forth an effort, that means that you have to have a direction that is beyond your existing point. If your existing point has you underemployed, then you need to put forth an effort that matches your employable skill set. If your existing point has you contending with depression, then you need to put forth an effort that uses therapeutic principles that provide mental wholeness. It takes courage to determine that you no longer want to be in a stuck position. I remember reading the story of Rosa Parks from *The African-American Book of Values*, compiled by Steven Barboza, and her recounting of her experience on that bus on December 1, 1955. She said, "People always say that I didn't give up my seat because I was tired, but that isn't true. I was not tired physically, or no more tired than I usually was at the end of a working day. . . . No, the only tired I was, was tired of giving in." It is important to understand that what we contend with in life is an opportunity for God to demonstrate his power and grace through our lives. What are you waiting for? It is time to move the needle!

The Recapture

Being flexible will cause you to . . .
Develop a powerful presence
Operate with purposefore
Put forth an effort where quitting is not an option

Chapter 11
Move the Needle

It has taken me more than three years to complete this book. I started writing at the time this country elected its forty-fifth person to serve in the Office of the President. Although externally I wanted to, I could not get past the rhetoric of this administration. I could not get past the racial tensions that currently permeate the fabric of our society. I struggled as a person of faith, as I watched those who named the name of Christ as Savior and yet disassociated themselves from the legacy of Christ through acts of bigotry and hatred. I was challenged—and remain so—in my own personal relationships in the communities of family, friendship, and faith. I battled guilty feelings as I watched dementia overtake my mother to the point where she does not realize that I am her son.

So, what did I do to move forward? I moved the needle. Like many people during the COVID-19 pandemic, I have been reading, resting, and watching old movies. It occurred to me during a movie-binging moment why I had not moved the needle on this book. I was watching *The Mission*, where a former slave trader, Rodrigo Mendoza, played by Robert de Niro, converts to Christianity; he struggles to climb up a waterfall dragging his armor (a representation of his former life of violence), only to get to the top and have a tribesman of the people he captured as slaves run up to him with a knife—and instead of killing him, he cuts him free of his burden. Despite the many changes and accomplishments in my life, I was still dragging the baggage of my past. I allowed myself to be weighed down by who I was and was not focusing on who I have become (and who I am becoming).

Let me give you three statements that I was reminded of recently: 1) Our past, sometimes good, sometimes bad, can hinder us in going into our future; 2) It's unfortunately awfully easy to go into the future while still being shackled to the past; and 3) Expectation without investment is just a wish.

Our past, sometimes good, sometimes bad, can hinder us in going into our future. It has been said that we often stand in our own way. When Moses sent spies to check out the land that God had promised Israel, only two out a delegation of twelve could muster a good report. Although they were no longer slaves, their past position was hindering them from seeing the promise that God had for them. Does that sound familiar to you? Are you blind to the promises God has for you? I mentioned earlier that I read the works of Charles Spurgeon daily. He says, "Advance beyond the dreary if; abide no more in the wilderness of doubts and fears; cross the Jordan of distrust, and enter the Canaan of peace, where the Canaanite still lingers, but where the land ceaseth not to flow with milk and honey." I love the prose and power of Spurgeon. I get energized by the images of his words. It is important to fuel your thought process with the proper energy that propels you to action. Proverbs 27:19 (NKJV) states, "As in water face reflects face, so a man's heart reveals the man." While your past does help to shape who you are, it does not have to be the determining factor in how you live your life.

It is unfortunately awfully easy to go into the future while still being shackled to the past. I view life as a journey that is filled with opportunity. I realize, though, that there are many people who do not share the same position as I do. Furthermore, I realize that some of those people are individuals that I am connected to on a variety of levels. Have you ever been to a family gathering (holiday, family reunion, etc.) and people in your family want to have the "I remember when" conversation? They want to remind you of situations and actions that were a part of your past. While some of these statements can be innocent, many of them can be painful. I had an uncle who regularly reminded me that I had accidentally killed his hamsters when I was five years old. But the story did not stop there. It would evolve into another incident and another incident about something that someone did in their past. Now, do not get me wrong; my uncle did not mean any harm. But the devil will use that as fodder to keep you in a stuck position. I know people who can't develop relationships because the shackles of their past are making loud noises in their heads. You cannot produce positive traction with negative energy or thoughts. When you choose to move the needle, you go into the future fully aware of things of your past. Yet, you move with a heart of peace because you know that those things do not solely make up your being. In his book *The Way of the Warrior: An Ancient*

Path to Inner Peace, Erwin Raphael McManus states, "The way of the warrior is a discipline of the soul. It is a journey toward enlightenment. And ultimately it is the outcome of a relationship with the Creator of the universe. The world in which Jesus lived never knew peace, yet no matter how hard the powerful tried, they could never steal His peace." If you allow it, your past will rob you of your peace. So do not allow it to cause you to focus on the bad or become content with the good.

Expectation without investment is just a wish. Many people are stuck and afraid to move the needle, but expect God to move on their behalf "in spite of." It takes courage to get up each morning to face your day when you have low expectations. Just the same, it takes courage to get up each morning to face your day when you have high expectations. The key to our success or failure is the amount of investment that we are willing to put into actions that can become better outcomes.

I intentionally get up each morning and spend time reading, reflecting, and releasing my day to God. It is an investment of time that allows me to hear God and to be heard by God. This investment of time is what strengthens me inwardly and outwardly. On many days, I am carrying the weight of the world (or at least I think I am) and managing hidden fears and concerns that I have for my family and friends. I have learned, though, that courage does not cancel out or dilute fear. Being strong means that I push through my fears and move forward despite my fear. I make this time of investment because I realize that God is empowering me so that my expectations are not just wishes. This investment of time allows me to acquire knowledge that aids me during my journey.

COVID-19 has created a place of endarkenment for many in our country. I have shared on webinars and in one-on-one conversations that the only way to arrive differently, having grown from the experience in the place of endarkenment to the place of enlightenment, is to not *get through* a thing, but to *grow through* a thing. Father Richard Rohr heads the Center for Action and Contemplation and offers daily meditations. In his meditation entitled "Dark Liminality," from April 28, 2020, he says, "It takes willingness, fortitude, knowledge, skill, and a deep trust in Spirit to go into these dark places as both witness and companion. . . . To heal from our suffering—not merely to ease or palliate it, but to transform it into the source and substance of our growth and wisdom—requires a journey through it." You must be willing to grow through challenges and circumstances so that you come out on the other side whole. You deserve to experience the things that God has purposed in His heart for you.

Over the years, I have used a principle that helps me to move forward from the things I face in my life. I call it the Resurrection Principle. John 20:6–7 (NKJV) says, "Then Simon Peter came, following him, and went into the tomb; and he saw the linen cloths lying there, and the handkerchief that had been around His head, not lying with the linen cloths, but folded together in a place by itself." It involves three things that happened after Jesus was taken down from the cross. There was a pity party, there was an executed plan, and there was a display of power. I use this model (depending upon the circumstance) for a period of three hours, three days, or three weeks. When Jesus died, the disciples had a pity party. Peter became depressed because of his action and they were all holed up in a room. So, for the first period of time I have a personal pity party (hour one, day one, or week one). I go through the emotions of feeling sad or being upset. The second phase involves the making of an operation plan. While the disciples did not see a plan in operation, God was already moving to the place of conquering death, Hell, and the grave. God had a plan. The third phase involves the development of power to transform the situation. Jesus took the time to leave the grave clothes in the tomb because God's power raised Him up from His dead situation. You have that same power working in you, and it gives you the ability to move the needle.

Sources

Unless otherwise indicated, scripture quotations are from the Holy Bible, King James Version. All rights reserved.

Scriptures marked GW are taken from the God's Word to the Nations®. Copyright © 1995 by Baker Publishing Group. All rights reserved.

Scriptures marked MSG are taken from The Message®. Copyright © 1993, 1994, 1995, 1996, 2000, 2001, 2002. Used by permission of NavPress Publishing Group.

Scriptures marked NIV are taken from the New International Version®. Copyright © 1973, 1978, 1984, 2011 by Biblica, Inc.™. All rights reserved.

Scriptures marked NKJV are taken from the New King James Version®. Copyright © 1982 by Thomas Nelson. All rights reserved.

About the Author

Joseph K. Williams Sr. is an ordained Baptist minister with over thirty years of ministerial experience. He is a community builder who is an expert at building collaborative relationships between government agencies, corporations, faith communities, and the community at large. He currently serves as the CEO of Bridge of Hope, which works to help companies understand community thinking, and as a senior program director with Enterprise Community Partners. Previously, he served the senior community as CEO of Emmaus Services for the Aging and as the state president of AARP DC.

Rev. Williams works to empower people and communities through guidance and resources that enrich their core elements. In his free time, he enjoys reading, writing poetry, playing golf, and spending time with his family. Rev. Williams is a native of Washington, DC, and currently lives in Upper Marlboro, Maryland. He is betrothed to Ivey Nycole; they have five children and six grandchildren.

Learn more at www.bridgeofhopellc.com

CREATING DISTINCTIVE BOOKS WITH INTENTIONAL RESULTS

We're a collaborative group of creative masterminds with a mission to produce high-quality books to position you for monumental success in the marketplace.

Our professional team of writers, editors, designers, and marketing strategists work closely together to ensure that every detail of your book is a clear representation of the message in your writing.

Want to know more?
Write to us at info@publishyourgift.com
or call (888) 949-6228

Discover great books, exclusive offers, and more at
www.PublishYourGift.com

Connect with us on social media

@publishyourgift

www.ingramcontent.com/pod-product-compliance
Lightning Source LLC
Chambersburg PA
CBHW071010080526
44587CB00015B/2407